hit 2

STRAIGHT*LINES*

Susan Ross, *Inuit Grandfather*

STRAIGHT*LINES*

Mary Frost

Mary Frost.

*To Mary
with every good wish*

PENUMBRA PRESS

This first edition is Volume 52 in the Penumbra Press Poetry Series. Printed in Canada. Cover art, *Inuit Grandfather*, is by Susan Ross, used with permission. *Straightlines* was designed and typeset by Rachel Lander, a student from Simon Fraser University, working as an intern at Penumbra Press with the support of a grant from the Book Publishing Industry Development Program (BPIDP).

NATIONAL LIBRARY OF CANADA CATALOGUING
IN PUBLICATION DATA

Frost, Mary, 1936–
        Straight lines / Mary Frost.
(Penumbra Press poetry series ; 52) Poems.
ISBN 1-894131-33-9
        I. Title. II. Series.
PS8561.R667S87 2003   C811'.6   C2003-901022-8
PR9199.4.F76S87 2003

The publisher gratefully acknowledges the Canada Council for the Arts and the Ontario Arts Council for supporting Penumbra Press's publishing programme. The publisher further acknowledges the financial support of the Government of Canada through the Book Publishing Industry Development Program (BPIDP) for our publishing activities.

FOUND POEM

At the Catalan poetry festival,
the third prize
is a silver rose;
second prize
is a gold rose;
first prize
is a rose.

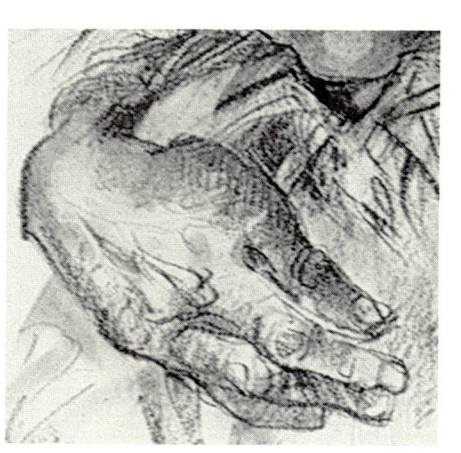

CONTENTS

A MATTER OF TIME

Circus, 14
Ritual, 16
Adolescent Summers, 17
Emma Observed, 18
Questions Concerning Fall, 20
Dinosaurs, 21
Things, 22
Still Life with Oranges, 23
Remembrance Day, 1998, 24
Angry Cat, 25
Time Check, 26
Break-Up, 27
Rake Dancing, 28
Clockwork, 29
On the Morning of Winter Solstice, 30
Summer Landscapes, 32
Snowman at Spring Equinox, 34
Late Autumn in the Garden, 35
Merry-Go-Round, 36
Plasticine, 37
Real Estate, 38
Journeys, 39
Flower Arrangement, 40
Strategic Retreat, 41
Star Song, 42

Forget-Me-Not, 46
Planting in Northwestern Ontario, 48
October Gladioluses, 50
Northern Bulletin, 51
Night in the North Woods, 52
Postcard to a Palm Tree, 53
Winter Carnival, 54
Tracks, 56
The Wild Geese Return to the North, 57
Bonfire, 58
Bush Garden, 59
Stone Terraces, 60
Dump Run, 62
Reed Island, 63
Frog Vespers, 64
Meditating with Murphy, My Old Black Sheepdog, 65
Our Topic for Today: Tent Caterpillars, 66
The Poppies, 68
Sea Breezes North of Lake Superior, 69
Excavated Rock, 70
The Honey-Gatherers, 71
The Green Canoe, 72
August, 73
Green Flamenco, 74
Walk Up the Hill With Me, 75

... AND OTHER POEMS

Yeats's Children, 78
Identikit, 79
Children of Lir, 80
Wordpower, 81
Jigging for Mackerel, 82
Sandblast, 83
Time Out, 84
Words to My Limbic System, 85
To a Dahlia Concerning its Intentions, 86
Mutant, 87
Inuit Grandfather, 88
Sleeping with Monet, 90
Rinpoche, a Tibetan Buddhist Monk, at the Unitarian
    Fellowship Hall, 91
Magi, 92
The Dreamers, 93
The Living Arctic Goes to the British Museum, 94
The Guy on the Garbage Truck, 95
Fat Cat, 96
Playmate, 97
Valediction for an Iraqi Girl, 98
Table in the Garden, 99
Sculpture on Wellington Street, 100
Caged, 101
Tourists on the Acropolis at Athens, 102
Visiting Greece, 103
Today at the Campsite, 104
Expedition, 105
Today, A Star, 106

Morning Meditation, 107
Comet, 108
Low Calorie, Sugar-Free Poem, 109
Firefly, 110
The Lilacs, 111
Housepet, 112
"Without," 114
Grey Moth with Orange Peel, 115
Once I Had Wings, 116
Up, 117
Wild Geese at Chippewa Park in Mid-October, 118
White Page Poem, 120

A MATTER OF TIME

CIRCUS

From the vaulted heavens, the Seraphim look down
on the splendid, circling circus of creation,
the pinwheel galaxies spinning
like Liberty ponies;
like a Viennese ballroom on a New Year's Eve.
From that viewpoint, our one-ring fit-up, Earth,
stands out blue and beautiful against the darkness.

The angelic hosts applaud our high-fliers,
capable of falling; their dare-devil insouciance
and their skill. The thrill of it
when success is not inevitable.

Aerialists, animal trainers, acrobats,
midgets, monsters, misfits
— we're all here —
musicians, ring-masters: but mostly clowns,
huge troops of us,
tumbling and at cross-purposes.

How the orderly heavens enjoy our chaotic options,
our comic capabilities!
Earth, clown school of the universe.
Leave it to us to get the belly-laughs.
Leave it to us to pull an audience in.
Cherubs at the concession stands
demand red noses.
They'd run away and join us if they could.

I have heard angelic laughter from the rafters,
the upper bleachers of the sky;
and the hush when, to a sad trumpet,
a lone clown leaves the ring,
slow shadow in a low spotlight
whose brightness tightens round him
like a noose.

For us as for fireworks, transience
is essence and pre-condition of our show.

RITUAL

A small girl crowned with daisies goes
singing along a winding path
marked out by double rows of pebbles
on bare earth.

In a grotto among the flowering currents, she celebrates
the obsequies of birds, insects, frogs.
Their matchbox caskets in her reverent hands,
she is priestess and mourner; and
the path's curves slow to ceremonious length
the passage to the grave.

All her later years, she hears,
round every dead wild creature that she sees,
her own voice singing, high and sweet;
and smells the bitter incense of
crushed flowering current leaves;

while Time by winding ways proceeds
relentlessly
with lonely ceremony.

ADOLESCENT SUMMERS

We collected seashells on the patch of shore
behind the crook of the pier's arm;
sifted through tangy gravel bright with seawater;
groomed rubbery tangles of the saffron weed,
expecting something exquisite —
a harvest of the exotic or the rare.

Surfacing through shingle,
long, disjointed rocks,
like skeleton hands, half-buried, half-exhumed,
reach towards the sea.

Out there, whalesong and dolphin depths.
Out there, the phosphorescent lure
of fish in silver shoals.

We combed the shoreline for cast-up relics:
cowries and conches,
white feathers from a tern's wing.
We carried them home and kept them
in a small box.

EMMA OBSERVED

It is indiscreet
and incredible,
this desire
shining in you.
It makes your skin
translucent and your step
airy as dandelion seed.

An apparition
unstable as a cloud;
a change in the wind
might deform you.
You beat in my heart, a dread
at such vulnerability;
so unguarded a stance.
I've been where you are
but underground.
The force you foster,
I repressed.
It became my igneous core.
The black seam
that I mine
chip by chip.
Desire bubbles from you,
an irridescent foam
airborne on every wind.

In my mind's eye,
I see you:
a passionate child
whose arms would hold the rainbow
though the world turned
and the weather changed.

QUESTIONS CONCERNING FALL

*"The sexual intercourse of angels is a conflagration
of the whole being." — W. B. Yeats*

This fire in the fall woods
burns like desire.

Is this the fire that wasted paradise?
Congress of earth and angels?
Rumours of flaming swords,
but were they drawn
in anger or in ecstasy?
Mankind and angels falling together?
Cadence each year and every life enacts?

Far from the green, unseasoned Eden,
every year a round of dalliance,
love and flagrant consummation.
Afterglow; winged departures; and a sleep.

DINOSAURS

For so long, only the bones.
Their survival and discovery
matters of chance.

The jig-saw wrongly assembled,
they were labelled slow,
cold-blooded, dull;
the brain inadequate
for the huge body. Now
the honey-combed bones suggest
they were warm-blooded, lively perhaps:
and some were colourful as jungle birds.

We dinosaurs ask you
when you read our bones
read carefully.
There is so little left
of what we were.

THINGS

Things catch their souls from us, our ectoplasm
insinuating itself everywhere.
As when the teapot is no longer just a teapot
but your aunt's teapot, bought as she left Finland alone
almost a century ago to come to Canada,
two sea voyages ahead of her and a land link to cross.
Something more than money invested in that pot.
Something more than tea pours from it now.

Is this why we want new all the time?
To be free of the soul-dust that collects around things?
Our bid on some correlative of youth?
Life, bright and uncomplicated as Pop Art baked beans:
unnuanced, born out of tin, no implications
of earth, of growth; no stain of the labour of gathering.
Bread-in-a-bag. No wheatfield. No millstone.
No spilled flour; no shadowed, appetizing kitchen.

We would avoid the spent, bedraggled selves,
our own and others', trailing back to roost
in the delapidated barnyards of our lives.
We sell up. We move to a small apartment.
Still things haunt us, moving in on us
like relatives with a claim to be cared for,
packing a cargo of connections
out of all proportion to their size.

STILL LIFE WITH ORANGES

Oranges in a cut-glass bowl. The bowl
spreads on the teak table a cut-light doily
of its own refraction.

The skin of the oranges coarse, the skin of peasants.
They sweat in the light, oily with effort,
missing the tree and the leaves' shade.

The grip of the rough palm is still with them —
the tug that tore them from the tit of the tree.
They must last now with what juice they have.

They feel themselves drying;
believe they will end
cut-glass.

They have wheeled out these swaddled centenarian veterans —
surely their last parade.
Returned to battlefields they do not recognize
since war is missing.

One remembers a crater.
Another the bloody guns.
Warrens of filthy alleys in the mud.
They remember bodies and barbed wire;
the smell of shit and bacon.

Now in the wind and rain,
they avoid each other's eyes,
the sight of what they've become.
It is better when they're lined up wheel-to-wheel,
where once they were shoulder-to-shoulder.

YOU ARE HERE TO BE HONOURED.
YOU ARE HERE TO BE GIVEN A MEDAL.
They nod, their eyes pearly and weeping.
They recognize the tone.

They know why they're here.
In bunkers of wheelchairs, rugs and plastic sheeting,
they are hunkered down and praying to survive.

ANGRY CAT

I have felt my mother
on my back,
claws digging in
above me.

The bunched and bluing puncture clusters
are less painful than the shock
of the distress that drives her;
her mostly-hidden rage,
that age grips her but has, as yet,
a lesser hold on me.

I kneel on the carpet
with my arm outstretched.
ready with stroking.

In the bones of my hand,
my own claws are forming.

TIME CHECK

She is lost
among the little plots of time,
the allotments
of hours and days.
Unwilling to accept
the simple fact of day,
the fact of night;
to set her life by hunger
and by sleep.

She adjusts her grip
on the day of the week,
and on the hour of the day:
her hold on the present.
"It is Sunday to-day, isn't it?"
It is Thursday.
"What time is it, exactly?"
It is twenty-two minutes past eleven.

Within minutes, she will ask again,
peering dimly at her watch.
She can still read it
but she doesn't trust it.
She reckons
it is losing time.

BREAK-UP

I remember when the ordinary words
began to desert her, stranding her un-
predictably in cracked white silences.

Her impatient fingers, snapping,
would have filled in the gaps if they could.
In those days, she knew who we were.

Today, I watched the ice-sheets craze,
panes part or over-ride each other.
On that ice, you could drive till recently.

Out at Black Bay last spring, the onshore winds
piled up glass mountains on the stoney beach.
The lake washed fretfully around their base.

Castaway syllables of frozen lake-song.
A brittle music, prone to landslides
and occasional soundlessness.

RAKE DANCING

Out of three feet of snow, sticks
the head of the earth rake I forgot to stow,
back in October.

January now; and the black enamelled tines
— strong, even teeth —
gleam in the sunlight
above the dazzle of snow:
a keyboard,
spotlit;
a broad smile;
a backyard cabaret
whose song is spring,
the earth breathing,
chorus-lines of flowers in pinks, blues, mauves,
bobbing and bouncing, on stage in all the borders.

I skip down the seven steps
from the side door to the driveway.
If it weren't for the snowboots,
I might dance —
pirouetting down a length of picket fence
towards a trellis twined with roses and sweet pea
— if it weren't for the boots
and the ridged ice under the snow.

I will change my woollen mittens'
double thickness of knit black
for fair-isle in flower shades.
I will trade my winter-white toque
for a fuzz of gold angora
like the sun.

CLOCKWORK

Time starts with spring.
The small cogs of the sky
wind up. Our music-box
starts its predictable tune;
we figurines
our predictable rotations.

I will ski all summer.
I will harvest tomatoes in March.
I will have the wild geese fly north
in late September.
I will set fire to the calendar.
toss my watch in the compost
and take a sledgehammer to the clock

You will find the clockworks of my garden
broken; springs sticking out of the soil.
Around our patio, magnetized dolls
with the disks of their feet to the sky.

Sun on my face, behind glass.
> Behind closed eyelids, everything
>> a swirl of flame and gold.
I am a body with a head of fire.
> I am the woman
>> clothed with the sun.
If the sun stalls,
> I can go on
>> to orbit in its stead.
It burns my face,
> shines through
>> the letter-boxes of my eyes,
illuminates the insides of my ears,
> the back of my skull,
>> the oubliette of my throat.
Fever of light in the emptiness of my head,
> the skin of my face crisping
>> from two directions.

Five hours ago, at Newgrange, dawn rays reached
> through the roof-box
>> of a pre-Celtic passage grave,
and struck the north wall of the main chamber;
> a once-a-year illumination
>> morning cloud can thwart.
That corbelled roof has held
> five thousand years.
>> What was buried there,

or placed in the basin stones,
          is long decayed.
                    Still, light returns.
Briefly the empty chamber
          fills with light; with light
                    and reflections of light.

SUMMER LANDSCAPES
Constable's "The Haywain" and "The Cornfield"

HERE, long shadows fall over the cottage by the elmgrove;
over the river and the riverside road
where a young dog runs by the ford.
Two dark Shire horses stand shank deep in the stream,
still yoked to the wooden cart. And the men,
who will not descend, rest in the horses' resting;
lean on the wagon-boards

And here, a boy has left his sheep to the care of the dog;
and tossing his cap on the grass,
lies over a stream to drink.
A high sun grounds in the gold of the corn
in the middle distance. On the path, the sheep
move through a patch of shade unhurried,
for the dog has stopped to watch the drinking boy.

It is the boy flung down full length on the ground
who alone has the measure of summer, its huge abandon:
his whole face burrowing to drink from the stream.

IT IS HE alone who makes hay in this pleasant season
where the trees take the long view
and the corn and the hay alike have an eye to the winter.
Only the boy, in his tantrum of thirst,
shines in the sun.
Something the boy knows, and the men have forgotten,
about water, or labour, or the purpose of summer.
Something the water gives to him only,
for the elms have outgrown it:
and the patient horses have no option on it,
yoked as they are; and the useful sheep,
with a path to keep to, seem not to need it.

I stand outside the frame of it all, in another country.
Find myself in the uneasy dog,
caught between two landscapes:
wishing myself again where the sun lights the water
and the small boy is lord of the long day.

SNOWMAN AT SPRING EQUINOX

"One must have a mind of winter"
— *Wallace Stevens,* The Snowman

Out on the lake ice, half a mile from shore,
naked of scarf, pipe, ceremonial buttons,
I am water standing on water.
My modular body and bald, featureless head
ought to have been of iron, cannon balls
in three stacked over-sizes — durable menace.
For months here, silent and sub-zero solid;
now, spring softens my brain.

Eyeless, earless, mouthless, without a nose,
I hear the dwindling moon, smell the wolf's speed,
feel the high notes of stars,
taste the mixed flavours of the northern lights.
I see the future and I am not in it.

The moon, my cinder goddess, fades in light.
I melt in heat, victim of old fire / ice
antipathies. Bitter to know myself
not the stern stuff I thought.

My head dissolves but the cold mind survives.
Do not imagine I will dance in summer water.

LATE AUTUMN IN THE GARDEN

Powerful in wellingtons, I move
between compost bins and bonfire, free at last
of failures that I've lived with all through summer
Cutting and clipping, I judge, move, banish
or let be — next year's garden already flourishing
inside my head.

I gather up the fallen haulms
of sweet peas that overburdened their supports,
a few, late blossoms lighting on them still —
copulating butterflies, caught in the act.

Leaves mottle the orchard grass.
Around me, happy autumn fields invite
tears and thoughts of days that are no more.
But I have little time for that,
busy and cheerful, totally absorbed —
like God after a world's end.

MERRY-GO-ROUND

Bright and blue, the music of summer
breezes out,
hurdy-gurdy tunes
for the white waves' prancing

Carved manes and gilded curlicues
and circling, mirrored canopy of lights,
the painted horses rise
and fall.

Fluted brass poles
spiral for ever up;
and penny-in-the-slot,
a copper sun sinks down.

Night rings
the tuppence-coloured fair.
Spilled rainbows bleed
into the hushed, black tide.

PLASTICINE

Tired of continuous mutations
and envious of the achieved,
I think of plasticine in small, tin boxes
in the tall, kindergarten cupboard.
Issued (one tin, one board, per pupil):
a reprieve from lessons, reading, sums.
Did Leonardo ever know a joy
to match our joy?

Out of the cold cupboard and the dull, dry tin
the plasticine came, as hard as stone,
its colours melded brown;
at most, a speck of colour here and there.

Puny pressure whacked it into compliance.
It took warmth from our exertions,
came to life.
We rolled it to a ball, a cylinder
lengthening and thinning it to fragile string.
We coiled it into disks, dishes, saucers, cups;
made outline flowers, houses, faces;
used it to form huge letters; and, when it ran out,
we squashed it back into a ball
and rolled it out again. When time
ran out, it was gathered up and put
back in the box,
back in the cupboard.

Since then, I've been
flower, face and house;
Now I am the mud string taking form,
and waiting for the hand to crush me round.

I have lived in twenty different houses.
That does not include holiday houses,
or the times I've stayed with relatives.

I used to want an Irish cottage.
White-washed stone walls, small windows,
reed-thatched roof;
beside the sea, beside a stoney shore
where sea-pinks shivered in the wind.
An orchard at the gable end;
hens scratching there; and on the orchard wall,
a black cat licking the sun off her fur.

I'd keep a turf fire on the open hearth,
with sugan chairs around the firelight's rim.
A bog-oak table, places set for eight,
on woven mats: red, saffron, purple, green.
Eating with me would be
like dining off the *Book of Kells*.

Oh well! Part of my heart
lives in that cottage anyway —
and pays no taxes.

Next move, I'll choose a castle
in the air. Too old to break new ground,
I'll rake the clouds: the sky, my Japanese garden
with a rainbow bridge. In the night woods,
great arm-loads of wild stars.

JOURNEYS

Stones that we trusted proved
unequal to the burdens that we placed on them.
The old gates close behind us;
dew-fired cobwebs chain and padlock them.

We walk between high walls, behind which
we suspect gardens, though we see no blossom,
hear no birdsong.
Strangers among strangers,
we put up steel shutters at our eyes.

We have travelled too many roads,
all of them leading away. Now,
wavering moonpaths offer
water to walk on towards a dark horizon.
Runways of stars are lit
for flights we will not make. We sit
in firelit rooms behind closed doors,
listening to the flicker of a few small flames
and the terminal purr of the ash.

FLOWER ARRANGEMENT

The members of the Garden Club are gathered
for their Christmas flower-arranging demonstration.
The Brass Logholder with Silk Poinsettias
shines on the raised hearth, a brilliant bauble.
Only the Fresh Chrysanthemums remain.
The tweed-costumed, grey-haired, energetic lady
with the efficient hands and strenuous voice goes on:

"Part of the beauty of this next display is
that everything is genuine plant material.
First, these two selected driftwood pieces
touched with a hint of silver here and there
to brighten the bleached wood.
One upright, one recumbent. There you have
the basic outline of the whole arrangement.

We'll leave aside the flowers to the last:
our bronze chrysanthemums will be the final touch.
Now, our foliage. This mahonia —
still dark and glossy green, still pliable, still prickle-edged —
this was a great success! Preserved in glycerine."

The mummified leaves grasp at her sleeve,
clutch at my heart and suddenly I see myself
as flower arrangement — recumbent,
lightly touched with spray
to brighten the dead colour.
And the chrysanthemums still added last.
I have leeched away into the plant material.
I stand
petrified.

STRATEGIC RETREAT

I have withdrawn into the fortress of my head,
my skull and its environs.
Crossing with some relief
the drawbridge of my neck;
abandoning
my ungovernable provinces,
my overtaxed extremities,
toes, fingers, hands and feet,
my pleasant, loved peripheries.
In this capital, I hope to pass
my winter years in comfort.

Yet, in occasional springtimes,
I want hands skilled in touching
to explore the young earth; and regret
I have no longer feet agile enough
to bowl along with giddy winds.
Sometimes I dream
of high adventure on mysterious seas
such as the old charts mark with
"Here Be Dragons."

STAR SONG

For Travis Jollimore

When I was young
I sang a song,
a song for the stars to dance to.
It seemed to me
they were all so old,
they might be glad of the chance to.

Now I am old,
they sing to me,
but the song they sing is mine.
I can listen
long hours to that;
it comforts me like wine.

For they are no older
now than then;
and I am younger than that again.
I shared my ephemeral youth
with them.
They share their age with me.

For the heart can dance
though the legs grow lame
and the heart can sing with the stars the same
on the wintry night
as it did in the spring,
swing round the patient moon and sing.

That Youth and Age
are the self-same thing:
"It's only a matter of Time," we sing;
and we welcome the day,
for the rest it brings.

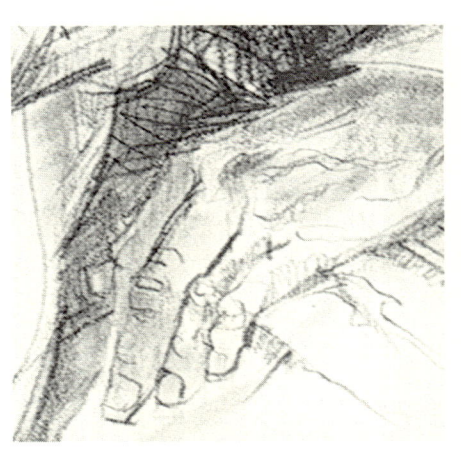

THE HOUSE ON THE HILL

FORGET-ME-NOT

I planted two forget-me-nots,
one pink, one blue.
They went wild and seeded everywhere —
in the terrace walls, along the stoney paths,
around the cracks in the driveway.
Green as lettuce; the flowering fleeting,
pale and unimpressive.
Forget-me-not.
Forget me not.
How can I?
You have me surrounded.

Poppies are more positive:
they say "Remember."

We stumbled into war,
volunteers or conscripts — does it matter?
We were enlisted, armed and in the trenches;
obeyed the orders that came down the line.
In the end, both wounded, we withdrew.

I survive in the bush
with a distant view of the lake.
A clearing backed by a granite hill.
The forest pushes in and I push back.
I get on better with the rock
which lets me be.

There are deer among the trees: I hear them.
However delicately they step, the dry wood snaps
They do not often move into the open,
elusive as memory

At the rim of the night, I recall you,
as I stand watching the self-seeding stars.

My garden spade connects with loss.
The wooden handle
cannot insulate me from it.

Lone men dug here
stopping and stooping to clear roots
and rocks, and they remembered the soft fields
plowed by generations of their ancestors.
Their silence and their sweat
informed the soil.

They cut down trees. Why
should the trees keep what necessity
had forced them to surrender? They honed
the edge of the axe, sharpened the saw's teeth,
on their own keen sense of loss;
and memory plagued them like a cloud of black-flies.

Even the woman with a dishpan at the door
flinging the dishwater out over the flower-garden,
acted less in delight than in defiance.
Wilderness would not be all. She
planted seeds of cultivation
beyond the bare necessities.

The Old Country bonded them
— even when it was not the same
old country. They had exile
as their common heritage.

In log cabins, they struggled to survive,
chinking the logs with moss. A den.
If life became too hard,
they gave themselves up to the trees,
hanging like spoiled fruit
from the supportive branches.

OCTOBER GLADIOLUSES

A first, fierce frost has blasted
the swords of the gladioluses.
Blades broken; others
ice-sheathed to the hilt.

Gathered in a vase, the blighted blossoms
drip thawing silk-juice
on the table's wood.
Splashes of flame and purple.
Ink and blood.

NORTHERN BULLETIN

We speak out of the dangerous quarter of the sky
where the circling sun runs underground.

Shaped from ice and darkness,
few syllables serve us.

Our repartee is slap-stick and breaks bones.
Our silence is thirty below.

Though around us the bright firmament wheels,
we dream of ravens leafing a winter tree.

There is a skunk out there. I've seen him,
elegant in white velvet and black fur,
in afternoon sun on the lawn.
I saw him again when the white-tail deer,
all nervous neck and nose and tentative hoof,
came close. The skunk played possum,
flat as skunk-skin discarded on the grass.
When the deer left to nibble lily-stalks,
skunk sauntered off, nose down, back arched.
His arched tail flowed behind him like a train.

The skunk is out there.
I can live with that — until, on Devil's Night,
the dog brings it home to me,
crashing through the door
to wipe his muzzle everywhere:
chairs, sofa, carpet,
me.

O my aromatic skunk!
He flavours everything:
my morning coffee and my sandwich lunch.
He dens in my nose. Parades himself
on the fine pebbled surface of my tongue
I have been marinaded twenty hours in skunk.
I have absorbed him. Now I exude him.

In the mall, I wonder
that heads do not turn as I pass.
The crowd should part before me, a Red Sea.
I am not merely skunked; I am skunk.

POSTCARD TO A PALM TREE

Palm tree, I am returned
to a cold world. White sky, white ground,
white walls of snow-laden bush. I am back
among stiff Presbyterian spruce trees
whose rectitude upbraids
your pagan abandon;
whose silence scores against
the urgent, ebullient, heart-pounding beat of your
drums.

In the back of my mind, like an echo,
your shadow is swaying on sand.

Late February and we have snow again.
Not salt, not feathers, a sustained slow dredge
of icing sugar, like we had yesterday
and had the day before. The sky is falling
Spoon it over ice-cream on a sponge base.
Three minutes in a hot oven.
How's that for Baked Alaska?

Years fell like this — mildly and over a long period
building up on my head.
Decades covered the roots.
Half a century hid
the strong, thick brown of my hair.

Around noon today, when the wind picked up,
the balsams threw snowballs at each other.
Every laden bough an arm with packed fists.
The grove a bunch of teenagers jostling each other;
wind rushing uphill joined them, piling on.

Now, it's the birches skinny-dipping.
A Finnish influence.
They beat each other with twigs.
And this is winter.
What will they do in spring?

I will fling off the years like blown snow —
a good shake should do it.

My white hair will recover its colour.
When run-off comes, I'll be a river of tears.
What cries might laugh.
We are not bound in stoicisms of ice.

TRACKS

In snow or in sand ground, they print
signatures I cannot read.
Record their size and speed,
and whether it was recently they passed.

I return to study their alphabet.
Tentatively, I pronounce this: BEAR.

I try on the bear's skin. Find it
a poor fit — the fur weighty; and the black
oppressive. Incompatible with
the feline in me. I have
sharp eyes and retractable claws.

I set the bearskin by. It leaves me
with a better nose; a new appreciation
of the bouquet of an apple.

THE WILD GEESE RETURN TO THE NORTH

Old dame with an old broom,
I clear the ground where the wild geese return.

High overhead — their call pumped by the wing-beats —
lines of them perforate the sky's blue underbelly.

Tear along these lines that they prepare.
The sky will split like a pinata, spilling summer:

flowers and ripe fruits packed
in the spiked straw of the sun.

BONFIRE

Let the bonfire be a funeral pyre.
It has already consumed
two four-month-dry Christmas trees.
In the first, wind-driven sheet-flames,
they went off like sparklers.
Pruned branches and off-cut lumber
took to transformation more sedately.
Fire changes things; let it change me.

I tend to the fire's structure
and its rim, careful to contain
its energies — surrounded as we are
by dry grass and old-growth forest.
I have a rake, a spade, a water-can.
After two hours, I'm kippered like a herring.
Dried, smoked and cured.
You could slice me and serve me for breakfast,
my flesh a smokey gold right through
and tasting of spruce.

Darkness. The fire has settled:
so have I. A winter jacket and a seat
beside the muttering, orange glow.
A poke of my rake sends sparks
wriggling into the night. Fire sperm.
May they beget constellations
at the edge of the universe.

BUSH GARDEN

A bush garden is the essence of empire.
Natives uprooted. Landed immigrants
brought in to take their place.
Inside the palisade, a higher culture.

Left to themselves, the plants might get it together.
That is not our intention.
We patrol the perimeter, armed with deterrents.
Around the beds, impose an unrelenting apartheid.

Parachute brigades
land on our razed plains. Subversives
tunnel underground. We grow suspicious
of songbirds and squirrels.
What part have they in the resistance?
We reckon they're making the drop.

Collaborationists whose growth we have protected
run amok. Loosestrife takes off from the garden
to settle the swamp.

We sit on the deck in the sun on our off-duty hours.
The peace we had planned for eludes us.
In moments of silence, we listen
to scutch snaking under the fence.

STONE TERRACES

Rocks, like tears,
stream down the face of the hill.
You can keep nothing.
Whatever is must pass.

This rubble in my yard
invites me to construction,
like a child's wood blocks,
or a jig-saw puzzle
whose guiding picture is mislaid.
It begs to be placed in context:
some appearance of purpose
to justify what it has endured so far.

I can be kind as moss and lichens are.
One-morning-a-week cosmetician
in this old-folks' home,
I arrange the deranged.
There is a limit to what I expect to achieve.

I build low, loose stone walls, not daring higher;
and barrow earth to give them purpose. They retain.
Earth is my alibi for the stone dams I build.

Hauling down the boulders from the hill
on a snow shovel I drag behind me, bent forward
till my back parallels the ground,
I am innocent and timeless as a carthorse.
Straining along my sides, my arms,
stretched to the metal handle,

are no longer bone and flesh, but leather, tanned.
and wood: the traces of my tackle, shafts of my cart.
I am a detail of the landscape, like the trees;
like sand or sky.
What I would choose to be is rock,
its spirit not immortal but enduring.

When I myself am broken, bring me here.
Give me a place on my stone-terraced hill.

DUMP RUN

By the shoulder of the highway, a small sign
says LANDFILL SITE — as if the cars and trucks
turning in every weekend are part
of some altruistic conspiracy
to heal a hole in the earth.

Along the dirt road off the highway, trees
are flagged with plastic grocery bags
that rattle in the wind.

The damaged playpen, the unstrung guitar,
old mattresses:
we haul the past out to discard it here,
its privilege of privacy withdrawn.
Now it is outcast, it is communal.

O give the gnome-like, squat custodian
a purple stole. Let his confessional be
his windowless, chipboard shack.
I will repent and leave my sins here too
with all the rest this place absolves me from.

Plough it all under, out of reach
of the gull's beak and of the black bear's claw.
The bear, another garbage bag among
heaped, ripped, black garbage bags
until he lifts his head; confronts me,
eye to eye.

REED ISLAND

After a week of rain,
the one reed island
in our bush pond
upped sticks
and drifted south.
It ran aground
on black silt
by the outflow creek.

Today, the reeds; tomorrow,
it might be the trees
taking off without a by-your-leave.
(I've seen the beavers' pencil stubs.
I've heard the raindrops
muttering.)

I want to put that island in its place.
Haul the canoe up the bush path;
bring grappling irons,
tow the reed patch back.
Too late. It has put down roots.
Now only a flood will shift it.

Its restless gesture
changed the shape of the pond.
We have a reckoning due,
the reeds and I.

FROG VESPERS

They might have been birds.
Do they think about that?
They were for all practical purposes
small fish, and they transcended themselves.

Now, after a day of rain
they are chirping from all the ditches.
A froggy symposium. I will fall asleep
to their shrill carousing.

This would be a good night to dream
a school of flying fish,
as green as parakeets
and given to warbling.

Listen. They swoop and dip
and turn in unison,
myself among them,
trilling away with the best.

MEDITATING WITH MURPHY, MY OLD
BLACK SHEEPDOG

Now when I meditate,
Murphy joins me.
I sit. He sits.
In the same sun,
we enter the same silence.
A few deep breaths. He flops
resignedly. His muzzle rests across
his right front paw,
or else he licks himself,
monotonous as a mantra.

We breathe together
slowly,
half an hour.
Sometimes his breathing swells
into a sigh.
Occasionally, he snores.
(Who knows what sighs,
what snores, he hears from me?)

Brother in black fur,
I value the simplicities we share.
You, I, the golden woods,
are we not one?
Together now, and soon
together gone.
Companion pilgrims
on a common road,
let us be still
and know that we are God.

OUR TOPIC FOR TODAY:
TENT CATERPILLARS

Today, I will write about tent caterpillars,
those loathsome legions marching east, devouring
the June greenery.
Foul mats of them on branches, tree-trunks,
house walls, wood-piles, garden furniture;
and seething clots of them on the north walls.
They cover the handle of the careless rake,
the leaning hoe, the garden spade.
They make the hose their highway.

On a remnant rose-leaf, see them spasm and strike,
spasm and strike again. From inside the basement,
watch them, massed on a screen or wriggling up the glass,
their hairy forms back-lit. Over the driveway tarmac,
a shredded leaf-meal mixes with the fluff
of poplar seeds. Wind rolls them into soft cocoons
like green-and-white cigars but loosely packed.

I will not write today about my old black dog
who has been put to sleep; or walk into the yard,
his territory. There, while I dug and planted
he guarded me — though even he
could not protect me from this base invasion.
Not even in his good days, which were gone.

Listen: they are dripping from the trees: dripping
like the aftermath of rain. Voracious hordes,
unlovable and unloved.

Yet these, too, are good animals,
who had no option on being beautiful black dogs,
but come pre-programmed to denude the woods.
To crawl and fall. To pick the trees' bones clean.

THE POPPIES

Splitting their green baize shells,
the poppies dreamily unpack themselves,
their scarlet parachute-silks,

their flaming palm-sized petals
smudged with black:
seed-stains of their black hearts.

In everything excessive.
Too big; too bright; too bold; too numerous.
A flagrant, fluorescent inflorescence.

On this June evening, in the light
of an impending thunderstorm,
under the smoky sulfur of the sky,

the poppies burn like torches.
Earth warns heaven
she'll fight fire with fire.

The fishing boats are in and tying up
alongside their wharf in Wild Goose Bay.
Half a mile inland, uphill from the lake,
I tell it by the screeching of the gulls.

Bent over at my digging,
clearing stones from sand,
I know the sky behind me
is full of the wide wheeling of white birds.
I work in my own shadow
with my back to the sun.
In my salt sweat, sea air.

So long as I do not turn around
or look, the sea and seashore
fall, like drifting mists,
out of the gulls' cries.
Gauze scarves:
blue-grey and white,
and sand scarves spangled
with wet stones and shells.

EXCAVATED ROCK

We planned to scoop
a garden pond
in sandy soil below the hill.
This grey whale-back emerged instead,
baring pale and vulnerable skin.
The instinct of my palm, to pat its flank —
and then my palm's surprise,
finding it unyielding, not blood-hot.

Crouched on its hump,
I am Brendan, early mariner and monk,
beaching his boat on the back of a whale.
mistaking it for a rock.

If I light my cooking-fire,
this island will roll forward and submerge,
roiling an earthy edge,
the tilted tail-flukes lifting.

Down through sand, grey clay, away
from the bulldozer's growling,
diving to silent refuge,
below the aspens' surf.

THE HONEY-GATHERERS

The bees on the pink *spirea bumalda*
beside the picnic-table
fill supper-time with images of lust.
They add a relish to our tourtière.

Swarming the newly-opened blossom,
with tremulous urgency fumbling
from one flowerhead to the next,
insatiable.

Such incontinent carnality
brings concupiscence into disrepute.

They're the wrong build
for elegant lechery,
more Fatty Arbuckle than Bond.
All appetite, no style.
These guys want their martinis
shaken *and* stirred.

I shall re-name this shrub
the bawdy-bush:
my garden's red-light district.

Listen,
the sound of honey.

There were weekends, even weeks,
at campsites. In the cream inner shell,
coils of rope, fishing boxes, tackle;
varnished paddles propped against the seats
of varnished wood and woven hide.
Murmuring evenings, figures
black against fire-glow; tents
lit from within. There were bright mornings
and misty mornings; the prow muscling
through strong water; or sliding through
on days when the water yielded.

Too heavy for easy lifting
to the roof of the car
for the drive to the river or lake,
the overturned canoe
rests now behind lettuce and onions,
a fibreglass berm,
blessed by the outstretched arms
of a rotary clothes-dryer.

In spring, frogs sing
in the run-off ditch
at the foot of a nearby hill.

AUGUST

Now summer darkens its green; leaves
shrivel into themselves, so tatters of sky
show through the birch boughs. The August bees
are less industrious; but one white butterfly
is lively as ever.

I eat dessert standing up in the raspberry patch.
I gather gooseberries for pies I do not bake.
Drink tea in the shade,
my sun-thirst satisfied.

Already red lamps glimmer
on the crab-apple tree.
Already a darkening wine
blooms on the plum.
Up on the high, fine
spire of the balsam,
the squirrels pick pine-cones
that come tumbling down
like Christmas ornaments.
The squirrels too falling ornaments,
scampering groundward through
the flickering branches.

From the top of a blighted tree
at the edge of the wood,
a crow barks at the sun.

GREEN FLAMENCO

June afternoon, but dark with cloud and rain.
The balsams toss their heads and flounce.
Each tier of their dark green
edged with a ruffle of a lighter lace.

They stand tall. I dream
black hair drawn back and fastened
at the nape. Arms rise like flames,
lifted by the wind's gypsy rhythms.

A troupe in passionate movement.
Fire flashing. Hands clapping.
Heels rapping
summer thunder.

WALK UP THE HILL WITH ME

How many more days will we get like this
before the trees turn gold?
Last evening, at the marina,
the geese were flocking,
but not leaving yet.

Walk up the hill with me.
Behind the house, up the grass path,
on past the point where grass gives way to granite.
From the weathered wood seat on the rock,
we can look out
above green tree-tops to the lake.
There'll be no white-caps on a day like this,
a day of light airs, chickadees, red apples.

I'll bring two glasses
and a chilled, white wine.

Now
is all we have
or ever had;
and it is all we need.

Sit with me in the sun
and drink to summer.

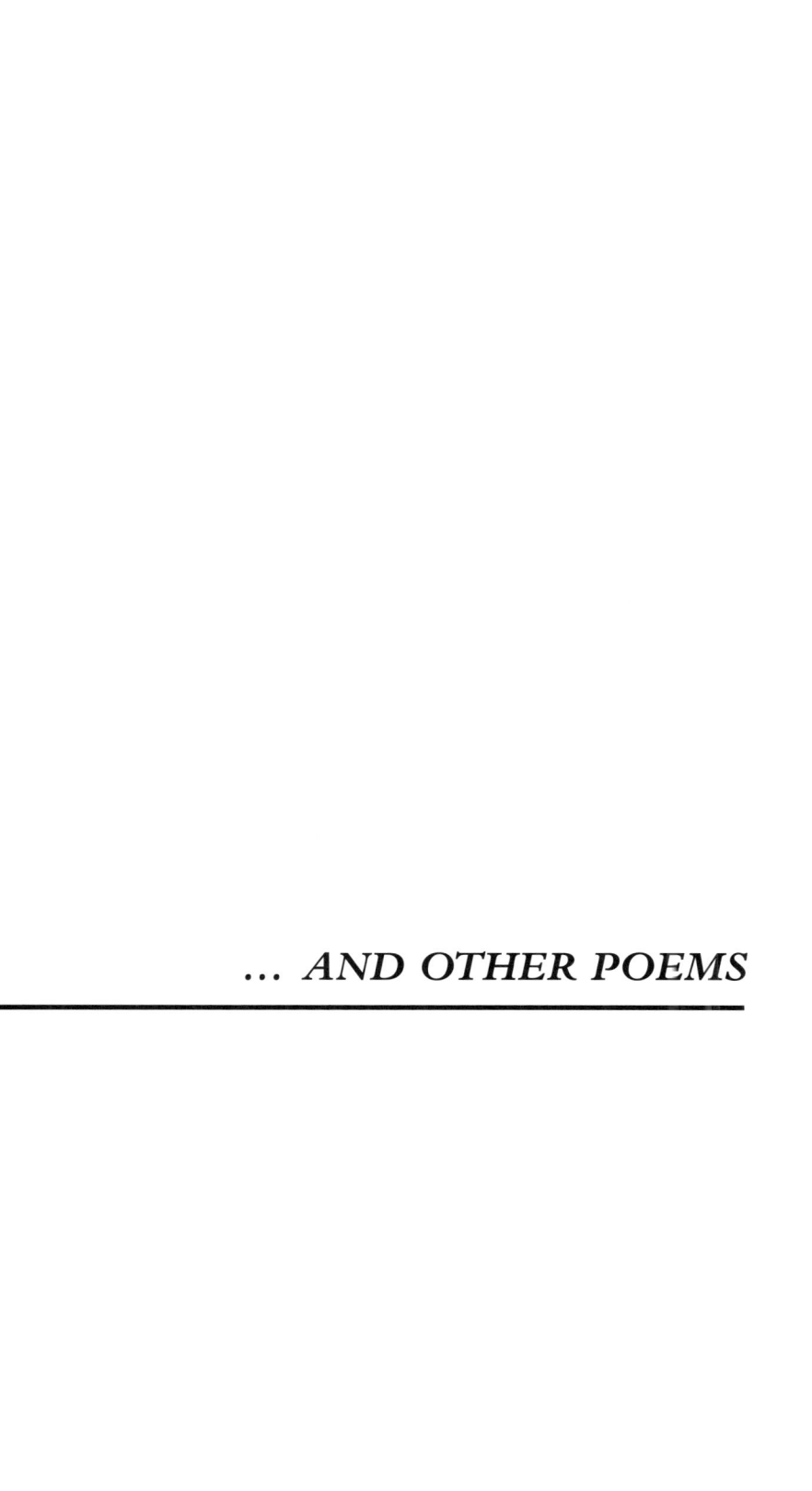

... AND OTHER POEMS

YEATS'S CHILDREN

Maynard tells the story
of how he visited Thoor Ballylee, Yeats's tower,
a Norman keep linked with two Irish cottages
in the loop of a singing river.

He walked a little up the country road,
found an old man pissing in a ditch.
and asked him if he had known Yeats.
He had. Indeed he had. Shure, everyone
living around there those times knew the Yeatses.
Before he tugged his bike clear of the hedge,
the old man made a cradle of his arms:
"Many a time," he said, "I held
his children in me arms."
And as he spoke, he seemed to rock their ghosts.

Maynard, telling that story to a group
gathered to read Yeats's poems, echoes the gesture.
He too has held Yeats's children in his arms;
he passes them to other arms to hold.

IDENTIKIT

I am the farthest echo
from a blue hill over the bay,
a landscape with sparse soil
where the alpine gentian finds
a frail hold between stones;
and sea-anemones open in salt pools.

From a cave in the mountain,
a rumour of bones.
Rain seeps from above.
In perpetual darkness, the floodwater rises,
filling the cavern
and the long passage into the rock.

Out on the hill,
a slab of stone hangs
balanced on rock pillars
and on the edge of the air.
Altar or ravaged tomb
where a famished wind
has eaten earth and bones.

I know those rock ribs
and the hollow heart.

CHILDREN OF LIR

The children of Lir, the Celtic sea-god, were bewitched by their
wicked step-mother, changed into swans and condemned to live
nine hundred years in that form.

True, it was sorrow then to leave our father,
but we were young and together.
To have wings was more than we'd dreamed of.

We took a grip on the air and rose.
The sea-foam simplified into white rings
that fringed the stain of the land. Sun
rested on our backs. We did not ask
again for our white arms.

Nine hundred years we had; our only music
what the wing-stroke swept from the harp of the air,
the flute-notes dribbling from the wing's tip
or bright notes streaming briefly
from the bat-black webs of our feet.

Nine centuries we lived with the winds
and the singing reeds and the passionate sea,
denied voices
till these last hours,
with only sorrow to sing.

"Earth," I say; and refine it:
"sand," "loam," "rock," "humus," "tilth"
I put ground under my feet.

"Trees," I say. I raise
jungles and coniferous woods at will.
I am the prevailing climate.
The climatic zones
are here in the back of my head.
I draw parrots from the pouch of my cheek
and ravens from my frontal sinuses.
I have bestiaries barred behind my uvula
that any zoo might envy.

My tongue
is a scorpion's tail.

JIGGING FOR MACKEREL

Hold the string
looped twice
around your index finger.
Let the wood frame of the jig
lie in the fish-sweet bottom of your boat.

Draw and slack.
Draw and slack.
Your arm is the line's pulse.

And the tug of the tide on the line
is an answering pulse.
Against its rhythms, attune yourself to detect
the flutter of something hooked.

Let your whole arm
listen for this response:
judge it nibble or bite.

If you land this fish,
it will come flavoured with salt air and sun,
the cries of the herring gulls
and the bucking of your small boat
on the back of the sea.

SANDBLAST

A smoky twilight
infiltrates and dissolves
the bare, grey woods.
In this light,
nothing is certain.

I envy the composure of rock.
I envy the resignation of sand.
Like sand, we are weary.
Like sand, we are formless.
Under scrutiny, there is some evidence
we've kept our edge. En masse,
we are conformable.

I am deciduous like the moon.
I have watched many times
over what seems my dying and rebirth,
not knowing surely was it I who died
or I who am re-born.
The transitional moment eludes me.

When there is nothing left to be said,
the music swells to carry the story off.
It ends in music, the only resolution.
Sand in the wind, but singing.

Pick up on the music early.
Learn to sing.

TIME OUT

This morning, I wish myself dumb. I ask
for a speechless season, to leave me
dumbstruck before beaded grass; before
light carried on the coal-black back of a crow.
I ask for a slow progress,
the way green mists the tree-tops.
To hold the moment in its essence only,
before the words' unfolding.

Frogs are singing and my heart keeps time.
An amphibian self has understood and replied.
I, too, have a home in the pond.
(I had forgotten.)

I have heard a listening
that is not the wind
holding its breath.

In syllables of silence, a new language,
I struggle to compose my response.
Against the weight of my own scoffing, I plod on.
I say what I have to say.

WORDS TO MY LIMBIC SYSTEM

My mute angel,
what have you learned,
patient through the wordy years?

Sometimes, I hear you humming,
I catch your echo in the willow's curve.
In the old days,
you were merry all the time.

With only music,
you possessed the earth.
Invested in the wind,
in water, light;
in what rose out of the ground.

Small sprite, I do not grudge you
your amusement.
Through the back of my head,
I see you doubled up with silent laughter,
pointing after me, as
with such dignity as I can muster,
I ride the penny-farthing
years and days
unsteadily,
to the cliff's edge.

What kept you going?

> While you burrowed underground,
> were your thoughts pink
> and circular?
> Did you learn stems
> from the earthworms?
> And from the earthworms
> did you learn to leave
> earth for air and sun
> and the sweet, strange feel of the rain?
> And having left, to leaf?

> Was green your first draft?

> How did you come
> to this perfection?
> To this exact
> number of petals?
> To that precise
> shade of pink?
> Did you make choices?
> (Did you think they were choices?)

When did you discover
your inevitabilities?

MUTANT

"I'm fine. There isn't a scratch on me." — *C.L.*

The roof of the red Acura peels
back the underbelly of the moose. He,
begotten of the catastrophic mating
of metal and meat, is born
in a shower of glass and guts;
his baptism, a sacrament
of excrement and blood.

While the beast above him
spilled its guts and dropped its soul on him,
he was granular and in transition.
He imagines that he stepped unscathed
out of the wreck, out of the moose-intestines,
back to the world of poetry and pie.

Creature of the waning moon's half-moon.
Bush soul. Night Being. Forest Spirit —
half man, half antlered god.
Myth masked as man, he troubles us
with what we had colluded to ignore:
our animal pedigree.

Licences have been issued.
Bands of hunters gather in the bush.
Civilized men are out there,
gunning for him.

INUIT GRANDFATHER
  A drawing by Susan Ross

The man is seated;
his small granddaughter stands at his side.
His right wrist rests on her right shoulder,
and his bunched fingers hold her parka
closed on her breast.
A large hand,
half the width of the child.

The face, all planes and angles,
a rock face,
relies on itself. His eyes,
hidden in the lines of puckered lids
— a glance formed against glare —
look down and off to the side.

I have known the ice too long;
the knife of the wind; a life
where night and day are seasons;
and want, the yellow bear,
is always on the prowl.
My faith is in the seal,
the spear,
the strength of my arm (which must fail).
We survive to survive.
Now, I live in a settled house
in a wooden town
and see a green world
on a small screen.

I join the hunt when I can.
I take care of the child.
I expect nothing.

The child, collared in fur
and open-faced as a daisy,
looks out from the arc of his arm;
is ready to smile.

SLEEPING WITH MONET

She sleeps with Monet
on the bedhead wall,
a panel of waterlilies.

He goes south with her in the winter.

On the bedhead wall,
as if the waterlilies
drip into her head
while she's asleep.

Graceful as water,
she carries
the pink and perfect
porcelain cup of herself.

RINPOCHE, A TIBETAN BUDDHIST MONK, AT THE UNITARIAN FELLOWSHIP HALL

Rinpoche, brown man in a grey robe, rises
to demonstrate walking meditation.
He lifts one foot, balances,
prowls it forward — a movement
barely perceptible.

Into my head's green space creeps
the image of a grouse.
One grouse. Five grouse prowling,
plumage of grey and brown.
Curled birchbark on dead leaves.

Dismissed, the flight of grey monks rises,
long sleeves flapping; clatters up
to settle in the rafters of the hall.
From there, Rinpoche beams down.

MAGI

So they were resin traders,
if you say so,
plying the camel route
through Bethlehem;
navigating by
the usual stars
or sidetracked by a comet.

Dealers in frankincense and myrrh,
their gifts to the baby,
his young mother, the new father, were
free samples,
though they added a few coins,
being prosperous and not ungenerous men,
who saw the circumstances.

On a regular business trip,
these men of the beautiful names
and dubious reputations,
who offered the first Christmas gifts.
They were traders
and maybe tricksters
but they were also kings
just as the folktale tells it.
When you act like a king,
you are a king.

Kings
recognize each other.

THE DREAMERS

At night, all his dead relatives
and some of the living, visit;
people he hasn't seen since he was ten
and total strangers with unusual manners.
He needs to wake to get some rest.

He wakes full of stories,
more drama than the newspaper,
impossible sequences and lots of travel.
I rarely get to go anywhere in a dream.
Once, I drifted down the Shannon in an open boat
without oars or engine. I wore a coarse, plain,
Cinderella dress in a grey-green,
a colour like old moss. When the boat drifted in
to a tree-lined bank, I stepped ashore
to a watermeadow with cows.
I only dreamed it once, but I remember
because after, I knew more about myself,
and how the river can take care of me.

I never dream about my father,
about my mother, who is still alive;
or Peggy who kept house for us for years;
or sisters, brothers, children or old friends.
Sometimes, in the mornings, when he tells me
how sociable his night has been, I'm jealous.
Why are my nights so solitary? Why don't my
dead relatives come visit me? Lately, I've wondered
if they ever really liked me much at all.

"THE LIVING ARCTIC" GOES TO THE BRITISH MUSEUM

The indigenous peoples of the Canadian Arctic
have sent these exhibits to London
in an effort at enlightenment.

The entrance is in near darkness.
Sounds of the polar winds.
In the distance, the lights of a northern settlement,
beckoning.

The English lady emerges to the top of the museum steps
suffused with smug revulsion.
"What appalling lives they lead!"
Tones of alarmed cockatoo
squawk in the undergrowth of her Home Counties accent.
"All I can say is 'Thank God for civilization!'"
And wrapping herself against the wind, she rushes off
into the half-light of the December afternoon.

She is followed by the disbelieving gaze
of a Roman ghost, a legionary
stationed up the road at Verulamium.
After a millenium and a half, still shivering;
still bundled in his cloak;
still stunned by the barbarity of Britain.

She doesn't see him.
She has never seen him.

THE GUY ON THE GARBAGE TRUCK

The boy on the back of the garbage truck
is in high spirits today.
He rides the step. His left hand grips
the handle at the side

It is February, but mild; sun on the snow
and on his yellow curls.

He waved when he picked up our black-bagged trash.
Now, riding the non-stop return run,
he leans back, waving to the world at large.
— a California beach-boy on water-skis.

It's the wrong place
and the wrong season,
but he's the right age;
and that is reason enough.

FAT CAT

In these crayonned pictures by child refugees,
the stick figures are clichés, except that here,
among the universal childscape trees,
the stick-men carry guns.
Lines of dots from the muzzles tie them,
unequivocally and forever, to the dead.

Yet none of this speaks as vividly to me
as does one innocent fat cat.
Improbably large and orange,
it glows in the courtyard of a great estate
that has many buildings and orchards.
Crouched down to eat,
its pink tongue links it to the dish.

It is not sufficient to show it.
The child supports the evidence with words
laboriously inscribed:
"In the house of the rich man,
the cat eats from a dish."

PLAYMATE

Somehow, the roots on the north and east sides
gave, and the lime-tree fell —
the uptorn disk of its base
raising a shield;
but half of the root-system held
so it did not die, but grew
prone, raised on the elbows of branches
and on the curve of its own spine.

It grew, part tree, part vine,
thirty feet;
not upward to the sun
but down along the shallow slope of ground.
Children,
who could not have climbed its height,
play in the branches
like birds
in the yellow sun
in the lime-green, yellowy leaves;
and they bounce in its spring.

It is their tree. They picnic here
lugging plaid rugs, canvas haversacks
with kitchen sandwiches and cans of pop;
and comic books to read
propped side-by-side against it in the sun.
It is their Dryad,
their Wood Grandfather,
come to stretch out beside them on the grass.
They are adopted into its green tribe.

VALEDICTION, FOR AN IRAQI GIRL

Drought was her inheritance,
the breath of a desert,
born poor and female —
a double disaster
even before the air
burst into blood and flame.

Close her wild eyes.

TABLE IN THE GARDEN

*A photograph of Henri Toulouse-Lautrec in the garden of his
mother's home in the summer of 1901, the year of his death.*

He is in a deck-chair. Dark suited; formal
despite the laid-back angle of the chair.
She, an unsmiling woman in a dark print gown
(long skirt, long sleeves, high neckline)
sits in a straight-backed, ironwork chair.
She wears an apron. Her left hand droops
in the draped scoop between her parted knees.
With shadowed eyes, she watches over him.
His height is not remarkable when he is seated.

The table which comes between them holds
tumblers and wine bottles. (One might be a carafe.)
Something of the café, if you stretch a point.
Something of escape in the garden air.
Something of absent friends in the three chairs
set back from the table around them.
A mother and her thirty-six-year-old son
together on a still, hot, afternoon.

In Montmartre there is music and dancing;
but nobody dances here.
We are a long way from the Moulin Rouge.
These immobile bodies
speak two grey tones of silence.

I scan the scene for flowers but find none.
Those mid-grey shutters at the windows might be green.
I would like to think they were red.

SCULPTURE ON WELLINGTON STREET

On a street in downtown Toronto,
I discover —
in the harried heat
of a July day —

a herd of cattle
sitting in the shade
of spreading trees
on a meadow-plinth between the tower-blocks.

Their metal curves as smooth
as fatted flesh.
Massive. Impassive.
Placid as Buddha.

Such ruminative repose,
the city's noises dwindle
to a buzz;
a gnat-swarm on a summer afternoon.

CAGED

Trees are naturally subversive
and inimical to the urban scale.
They impose a sense of proportion.

Banished from the overshadowed streets,
some specimens survive
imprisoned under glass
where neither wind nor rain can reach them.
Imagined voices of caged linnets.
(This is not their usual song.)

In the brownstone ghettoes,
remaindered blossom-trees.
The morning sun, re-oriented,
shines from the west,
out of the sky-high cages,
the glass tower-blocks.

Desperation on the point of breaking through.
The façade cracking;
torrents of mirror shards
and layers of bodies
hurtling into the streets.

Imagine what it must have been
in its heyday,
its gold and marble
opulent as the latest shopping mall.

Imagine the statue of Athena Parthenos,
chryselephantine,
smiling down on us.

The broken stones suffer us,
another army,
an interruption of the light
with which they have
a long-standing relationship

We'd like to pay our own small tribute here,
words like Pentelic marble
drawn from a distant hill
but we dare no such offering, over-awed
by the Parthenon's serene,
and well-proportioned "I,"
insistently repeated:
I I I I I . . . .

VISITING GREECE

A visitor's visa is not enough: I want
a black dress. A black scarf;
and an old man to shout at.
My own wine, my olive grove,
my mule. I need
a house built into a hillside,
whose darkness is my own,
with a heavy wooden door
to seal it in. A roof-top terrace
full of blinding light
for my eyes only. A courtyard
where a vine or lemon tree
spreads itself like a protective wing.

I need these stray dogs and cats
looking to me for sustenance.
They give me
temporary resident status,
do not disdain me
as a tourist passing through.

TODAY AT THE CAMPSITE

You were the only cloud on the horizon.

The lake glittered;
the birch trees whispered
of summer.

A patch of white bunchberry blossoms
in their own shy way
urged peace.

You set the lounger there
and crushed them.

You lay there,
sullen as Satan
and as ugly as sin.

Today at the campsite,
you were a black cloud
brooding over us.

Against you,
the forest's amnesty
could not prevail.

EXPEDITION

Love is an epic journey
into the interior:
always dangerous country.

You search for a lost city.
Your destination
is only a rumour.

The route is unpredictable
so be prepared
to live off the countryside.

When you arrive, if you arrive,
you will find it
already in ruins.

Out of the heart's rain-forest
rises
a pyramid temple

where flights of steps
lead up
to a ceremonial altar.

Do you imagine
you are summoned there
as priest?

TODAY, A STAR

Today, don't look for me to hold your hand.
Today, I am distant. I woke up a star
My light moves towards you.
When it strikes your eye,
you'll see me.

I am given to such transformations —
a hare; a star. To temporal dislocations —
I'm here today and then I'm here
tomorrow or yesterday or twenty years ago.
So it's no use talking to me about
the weather or the cost of living.
I know the cost of living well enough.

I don't make these changes. I am changed.
And on the chessboard of the Here-and-Now,
the move that I make depends on the piece that I am.
A bishop: I sidle. A knight; I leap.
Today, I am a star — a speck
of cold, gold fire, far off
and visible only in darkness.

Why would you want
a thing like that
on your hands?

MORNING MEDITATION

I close my eyes
on morning stars
a crescent moon,
moonshadows
and withdraw
where also stars are shining
and the moon
and the risen sun.

Looking for the point
where luminous winter holds
all seeding, flowering, harvest
in repose,
as white contains
the fan of the rainbow,
closed.

I am learning to sit,
to occupy my space
absolutely
like an oak tree.
No thought of going anywhere.
No thought.
Like wind in the branches, my breathing.

There is a coming and going around me.
I remain and become.
Winter overtakes me.
Bare tree
exact as a fishbone
against the silver tissue of the sky.

COMET

There you are, my lovely fly-by-night,
with the long hair streaming after you.

O my Rapunzel, let your hair down for me
and I will climb the night sky
and go and beg the galaxies with you.

You for my fire, my gypsy girl,
in the far, cold camps of the universe.

LOW-CALORIE, SUGAR-FREE POEM WITH NO CAFFEINE AND LESS THAN TEN PERCENT FAT

Apostles of dietary rectitude
correct us.
High priests of orthodontistry
make straight the bite of the horde.

When my cardiovascular system
is toned to perfection;
when my musculo-skeletal system
is supple in the highest degree;
when my cholesterol is pitched precisely
at the optimum point,
I will join the New Immortals.

I will jog through deserts of eternity
aware of nothing but my own pulse,
one of a long stream of the elect
all ignoring each other.

We will lap the universe forever,
our skin eternally flawless,
our smiles fully-furnished
and fixed.

FIREFLY

I am a firefly
on my way to the sun.

Such a vast distance.
Such inadequate wings.

Yet this a journey destined to completion,
for I am part of the shining.

THE LILACS

Driving the highway
in early June,
I wind the windows down
to smell the lilacs.

Cut-down and rooted-out,
lilacs in full bloom crowd
the back of the truck ahead,
en route to the landfill site.

The truck's hard springing
bounces them
as it rattles along:
a hard music to dance to.

They nod and wave and perfume the air.
A valiant gaity.
Courtesans in a tumbrel.
As good as dead.

HOUSEPET

The cat's dish —
scruffy as a sneaker on the outside;
its twin bowls licked smooth
and shiny as eggshell halves,
is everywhere:
under my feet,
by the stove,
in the toe-spaces below the kitchen cupboards,
screeching away from me across the vinyl floor.

Under my feet
like the cat ought to be
but isn't.
(He's in the basement, under the spare bed.)
The dish lies about and reminds me
of the strong claws
that will pluck the harp
of the backdoor fly-screen
tomorrow at six a.m.
and every morning till Doomsday.

One day, instead of screeching
when I kick it,
this dish will arch and spit.
One of these evenings at supper-time,
it will purr
and butt its head against my shin-bone
and rub its plastic skin against my ankles,
smoothly,
around and around.

I will feed it
chopped cat.

Next morning,
I will sleep in.

"WITHOUT"

Reading "Without," Donald Hall's poems about the death of his wife, Jane Kenyon

This grief
widows me,

"Without" —
a lack unlimited by any object.

I sit in the coffee shop, uncoupled:
an unclosed parenthesis;

a late phase of the moon.

The dead moth on the beige carpet
by the skirting board —
delta-winged,
flightless and noiseless,
is defined by lack.
Night finally got to him.

I pick him up as gently as I can
examine the wings' edging of dark spots
and scallops. One brittle wing
breaks off. Its underside.
less faded, not so dusty-pale.
Below that wing, another — fresher yet.
Power in reserve.

I end with a dis-assembled moth-kit in five pieces:
the two-inch torpedo head-and-body piece,
soot-streaked above and creamy fur below.

On the breakfast table, a mandarin orange peel
still in one piece. This pale, dismembered thing.
That colour.
I place the pieces in, close the skin round,
and close my hand around them,
willing a fresh pupation.

For all things dry and grey, I pray
for transformation. Some re-emergence
in a summer grove
to night flights scented with orange blossom.

Statues of angels wake my discontent;
and flights of geese,
a longing edged with envy.
Once I had wings:
my shoulder blades
and the long muscles of my back
remember.

I spread my arms out — see?
This is all I have left.

My soul flies up and hovers with the hawk.
My soul consorts with spirits.
When she comes back,
she tells me nothing.

We sit in the sycamore's shade,
at a time of her choosing,
reviewing what bodies know:
rainbows and river song,
the scent of thyme,
the warmth of skin on skin,
the taste of lemons.
I offer words, like jewelled goblets,
for her breath to fill.
We drink milk and we drink wine
together. Our symposium makes
a place for song.

UP

Stars in our eyes,
we climb our little ladders
towards the stars.
They end in clouds,
the stars as far as ever out of reach. We weep
star splinters; we come back
to earth. We work
all points of the compass;
we go deep.

Over us,
the long view, unattainable,
brightens and darkens. Stars blink
off and on. Winds tease out
vapour trails in a blue sky.
They spread and shred and vanish;
while on the wire fence by the garden shed,
the morning glories open blue umbrellas.

Haze offers some relief.
It lifts. Our hearts
(which are slow learners) lift

and we look up.

WILD GEESE AT CHIPPEWA PARK
IN MID–OCTOBER

The Brent geese, chin-strapped,
pin-headed,
large-bodied and long-necked
drift — seem to drift —
on the grey lake,
a brown flotilla
practising formations.

They ignore the tails-up ducks
among them
and the one agitated gull
that wheels and screeches,
picketing the beach,
noisier than all the geese together.

One by one,
they put aground on the sand-spit,
rear on web-tip,
stretch up necks and beaks,
spread out their circumflexed wings,
flap them like wind-snapped laundry.

They relapse
into compact goose-shapes,
waddle ashore and stand about in the breeze,
solid as sandcast ornaments.

But that one, winged moment
shook off
approaching winter with its snows
and claimed
the long sky,
a less-diminished sun.

The poem I can't write is a blank page.
It takes time to peruse.
It bears re-visiting. Memorize it
or carry it in your pocket, folded,
Stopped in a traffic jam or by a lake,
it will admit of different interpretations.

It is also a map:
a diagram that shows the core,
the courtyard, round which you are raised.
Dowse there with a forked twig to find
a spring. The possibility of fountains.
Cloisters. A walled garden.

Accept the blank page.
Please study it.
Although it does not bear my signature,
it is key to everything I write
Think it anonymous; or, if you care to,
sign it and make it yours.

 The cover of the book shows *Inuit Grandfather*, a drawing by Susan Ross. The drawing is of an Inuit man and his young granddaughter and is the subect of one of the poems. It is a picture of strong polarities: youth and age; innocence and experience; trust and wariness. He is granite; she is a flower. (See how the fur collar of her jacket translates into a circle of petals.) He looks sideways out of the picture; she glances up and looks out from the picture with a strong sense of seeking eye-contact. Though the drawing is the subject of only one of the poems, the polarities are relevant to many of them. Both the harshness and the sweetness portrayed in the drawing are in the book – as they are in the northern experience that inspired so much of it.

"At last, a volume of poetry by Mary Frost. Her voice has stayed with me for years. These stunning poems combine the holy and the everyday. The language is luminous and here we are, along with Frost, touching the mystery of time and life. Her sense of humanity is great. One can only say "thank you" for these words and lines and for the images that show something so perfectly true, recognizable at once as something we have always known. A teapot carried over from Finland, an old soldier on Remembrance Day, children on the shore: all are transformed by this poet's magic. A wonderful book of exquisite poetry."

—Veronica Ross, former writer-in-residence in Thunder Bay

"Ireland gave Mary Frost song and the landscape of Celtic legend. The Canadian Shield has contributed spareness to her wise and feisty poems.

For years, reading her poems in manuscript, I have considered her the most accomplished poet in Canada and Ireland to be without a book. *Straightlines* is some debut!"

— Claude Liman, Lakehead University

Discover and explore poetry with the
PENUMBRA PRESS POETRY SERIES
See website for complete list
www.penumbrapress.ca